ANIMAL BASED DIET COOKBOOK

Easy and Tasty Recipes to Help the Modern Carnivore Achieve Weight Loss and Vitality.

CHRISTIANA WHITE

GAIN ACCESS TO MORE BOOKS

DISCLAIMER

The recipes in this cookbook are provided for informational purposes only and are not intended as medical or professional advice. While the author and publisher have made every effort to ensure the accuracy and effectiveness of the recipes, they are not responsible for any adverse effects r consequences resulting from the use of the suggestions herein.

The information in this cookbook should not replace professional advice. Readers are advised to consult a healthcare provider or a culinary professional before making any significant changes to their diet or cooking practices.

Nutritional information is approximate and should be used as a guide only. Variations may occur due to product availability, food preparation, portion size, and other factors.

The author and publisher disclaim any liability in connection with the use of this information. It is the reader's responsibility to determine the value and quality of any recipe or instructions provided for food preparation and to determine the nutritional adequacy of the food to be consumed.

ABOUT THE AUTHOR

When it comes to tasty and nutritious cookbooks that turn wellness into a delightful journey, Christiana White is the author you turn to. She approaches cooking from a new angle and has a passion for creating wholesome food.

Motivated by her own pursuit of health, Christiana's books on Amazon are brimming with delectable recipes that demonstrate that eating healthily can be both simple and enjoyable. Her creative method makes cooking approachable to all skill levels by fusing entire, simple foods with flavors from around the world.

Readers of Christiana's meals gush about the beneficial effects her foods have on their lives outside of the kitchen. Her books are more than just recipes; they're guides for a happier, better way of life, resulting in everything from more energy to a revitalized passion for cooking.

Come along with Christiana to discover how to turn your meals into satisfying and joyful experiences. Discover the delightful intersection of health and flavor by delving into the colorful world of her cookbooks.

TABLE OF CONTENTS.

INTRODUCTION

Welcome to the Animal-Based Diet Cookbook, your comprehensive guide to living a life that celebrates the richness and diversity of animal-based nutrition. Whether you're an experienced carnivore or just interested about the advantages of an animal-based diet, this cookbook will inspire, educate, and satisfy your taste buds.

Imagine a diet that not only fills your appetite but also provides your body with the nutrition it requires. An animal-based diet contains high-quality proteins, healthy fats, and essential vitamins and minerals. It is a way of eating that has been adopted by many people who want to improve their health, energy levels, and overall well-being.

This cookbook contains a wide selection of dishes to meet all of your culinary demands. From hearty breakfasts to filling dinners, savory snacks to decadent desserts, each recipe is designed to help you enjoy every meal while adhering to an animal-based diet.

Are you ready to embark on a gastronomic adventure that will satisfy your taste buds while simultaneously nourishing your body? Dive into the Animal-Based Diet Cookbook to explore the delectable possibilities. Whether you're cooking for yourself, family, or guests, these recipes will impress and satisfy.

Join the thousands who have already discovered the advantages of an animal-based diet. Let's start cooking and make every meal a celebration of health and flavor!

CHAPTER 1: WELCOME TO THE ANIMAL-BASED DIET

Benefits of an Animal-Based Diet:

• Nutrient Density: Animal-based meals are extremely nutrient dense, containing critical vitamins and minerals such as B12, iron, zinc, and omega-3 fatty acids, all of which are important for overall health.

- High-Quality Protein: Animal products provide complete proteins, which include all of the key amino acids required for muscle growth, repair, and overall body function.

- Increased Satiety: High-protein and high-fat animal meals keep you satiated for longer, lowering the risk of overeating and aiding in weight management.

- greater Mental Clarity: Many people report greater mental clarity and cognitive performance after adopting an animal-based diet, which is most likely due to the absence of processed foods and the addition of brain-boosting nutrients.

- Stable Blood Sugar Levels: An animal-based diet can assist to regulate blood sugar levels, lowering the risk of diabetes and other metabolic problems.

- Reduced Inflammation: By avoiding processed meals and focusing on nutrient-dense animal products, many people notice less inflammation and associated symptoms.

- Improved Digestive Health: Some people report that eating an animal-based diet improves their digestive health, reducing bloating, gas, and irritable bowel syndrome.

- Increased Energy Levels: An animal-based diet's high nutrient density and balanced macronutrient profile can provide sustained energy throughout the day.
- Improved Body Composition: Because of the high protein intake and moderate carbohydrate consumption, many people who follow an animal-based diet report improved muscle tone and lower body fat.
- Simplicity and Satisfaction: An animal-based diet is simple to follow, emphasizing full, unadulterated foods that are both satisfying and tasty.

Common Misconceptions.

- Nutrient Deficiency: It is a prevalent misconception that an animal-based diet depletes critical nutrients. In truth, it contains a variety of vitamins and minerals required for good health.
- High Cholesterol and Heart Disease: Many people assume that eating animal fats causes high cholesterol and heart disease. However, current research suggests that dietary cholesterol has little effect on blood cholesterol levels in most people.
- Environmental Impact: While industrial farming practices can be damaging, sustainable and regenerative farming systems have the potential to drastically minimize animal agriculture's environmental impact.
- Expensive: Some people believe an animal-based diet is costly. However, by focusing on nutrient-dense cuts of meat and organ meats, it becomes more economical and cost-effective.
- Lack of Variety: There is a misperception that an animal-based diet is boring. In fact, it contains a wide range of meats, organs, dairy products, and even low-toxicity fruits and honey.

- Difficult to Follow: Some people believe that eating an animal-based diet is difficult to stick to. With appropriate planning and an emphasis on simple, whole meals, it can be straightforward and fun.

- Unhealthy Long-Term: Some say that an animal-based diet is unsustainable in the long term. However, many people thrive on this diet for years, reaping long-term health benefits.

- Ethical Concerns: While ethical concerns regarding animal consumption are justified, purchasing ethically grown and sustainably sourced animal products can help to solve these difficulties.

- Protein Overload: It is a common misconception that eating too much protein is unhealthy. Most people benefit from consuming a lot of protein from animal sources because it helps them maintain their muscle mass and overall health.

- No Fiber: While an animal-based diet is low in fiber, many people find that it does not cause digestive problems and may even improve gut health.

Getting Started: Tips and Tricks

- Make a slow transition to an animal-based diet to allow your body to adapt. Begin by adding more animal products and decreasing processed foods.

- Prioritize High-Quality, Ethically Sourced Animal Products. Consider grass-fed, pasture-raised, and wild-caught choices.

- Include Organ Meats: Organ meats are nutrient dense. Incorporate liver, heart, and kidneys into your diet to enhance your vitamin and mineral levels.

- Balance Your Plate: Include a variety of muscle meats, organ meats, and animal fats. This offers a full nutrient profile.

- Stay Hydrated: Drink plenty of water and try bone broth for extra electrolytes and hydration.

- Experiment with Recipes: Try new cooking methods and recipes to make your meals more interesting and pleasurable.

- Plan Ahead: Meal planning and prepping might help you remain on track and resist the lure of processed meals.

- Listen to Your Body: Pay attention to how your body reacts to certain foods and adjust accordingly. Everyone's needs are unique.

- Be Patient: Allow your body time to adjust and don't be disheartened by early setbacks. The advantages of an animal-based diet frequently become more evident with time.

CHAPTER 2: BREAKFAST

Carnivore Waffles

- Servings: Two.
- Prep time: 10 minutes.
- Cooking Time: 10 minutes.

Ingredients

- Four big eggs.
- 1/4 cup of beef gelatin powder.
- One-quarter cup collagen powder
- One-quarter cup water
- 2 tablespoons melted ghee or butter.

Instructions

- Preheat the waffle iron.
- In a blender, mix together the eggs, beef gelatin powder, collagen powder, water, and melted ghee or butter. Blend until smooth.
- Grease the waffle iron with a little ghee or butter.
- Pour the batter into the waffle iron and cook for the manufacturer's recommended time, usually 3-5 minutes, until golden brown and crispy.
- If wanted, serve hot with more butter or bacon on the side.

Nutritional Information: Calories: 250; Protein: 20g; Fat: 18g; Carbohydrates: 0g.

Liver and Bacon Omelet

- Servings: Two.
- Prep time: 10 minutes.
- Cooking Time: 10 minutes.

Ingredients

- Four big eggs.
- 100g coarsely chopped beef liver.
- 4 pieces of bacon, diced
- 2 tablespoons heavy cream.
- Add salt and pepper to taste.
- One tablespoon of ghee or butter.

Instructions

- Cook the chopped bacon in a pan over medium heat, until crispy. Remove and set aside.
- Cook the chopped liver in the same skillet until browned, 3-4 minutes. Remove and set aside alongside the bacon.
- In a bowl, combine the eggs, heavy cream, salt, and pepper.
- Heat ghee or butter in a pan over medium heat. Pour in the egg mixture, and heat until the edges begin to firm.
- Place the cooked liver and bacon on one half of the omelet. Fold the remaining half over the filling and cook until the eggs are completely set.
- Serve hot.

Nutritional Information: Calories: 350; Protein: 28g; Fat: 25g; Carbohydrates: 2g.

Sausage & Egg Muffins

- Servings: six muffins.
- Prep time: 10 minutes.
- Cook time: 20 minutes.

Ingredients

- Six big eggs.
- 200-gram ground pork sausage
- One-quarter cup heavy cream
- Add salt and pepper to taste.
- 1/4 cup of shredded cheese (optional).
- One tablespoon of ghee or butter.

Instructions

- Preheat the oven to 350°F/175°C. Grease the muffin tray with ghee or butter.
- Cook the ground pork sausage in a pan over medium heat until browned. Drain any extra fat.
- In a bowl, combine the eggs, heavy cream, salt, and pepper.
- Distribute the cooked sausage evenly between the muffin cups. Pour the egg mixture over the sausages.
- If using, sprinkle with shredded cheese.
- Bake for 15-20 minutes, or until the eggs are cooked and a toothpick inserted in the center comes out clean.
- Allow to cool slightly before removing from the muffin tray. Serve warm.

Nutritional Information: Calories: 200; Protein: 15g; Fat: 15g; Carbohydrates: 1g.

Beef and Egg Breakfast Bowl

- Servings: Two.
- Prep time: 10 minutes.
- Cooking Time: 10 minutes.

Ingredients

- 200 grams ground beef
- Four big eggs.
- One-quarter cup heavy cream
- Add salt and pepper to taste.
- One tablespoon of ghee or butter.

Instructions

• Cook the ground beef in a pan over medium heat until browned. Season with salt and pepper. Remove and set aside.

• In a bowl, combine the eggs, heavy cream, salt, and pepper.

• Heat ghee or butter in a pan over medium heat. Pour in the egg mixture and scramble just until set.

• Divide the scrambled eggs into two bowls. Top with cooked ground beef.

• Serve hot.

Nutritional Information: Calories: 400; Protein: 30g; Fat: 30g; Carbohydrates: 1g.

Creamy Shrimp with Eggs

- Servings: Two.
- Prep time: 10 minutes.
- Cooking Time: 10 minutes.

Ingredients

- 200g shrimp, peeled and deveined.
- Four big eggs.
- One-quarter cup heavy cream
- Add salt and pepper to taste.
- One tablespoon of ghee or butter.

Instructions

- In a skillet, melt the ghee or butter over medium heat. Cook the shrimp until pink and opaque, about 3-4 minutes. Remove and set aside.
- In a bowl, combine the eggs, heavy cream, salt, and pepper.
- Add the egg mixture to the skillet and heat, stirring gently, until the eggs are just set.
- Return the cooked shrimp to the skillet and stir until combined.
- Serve hot.

Nutritional Information: Calories: 300; Protein: 25g; Fat: 20g; Carbohydrates: 1g.

Organ Meat Pie

- Serves: 4
- Prep time: 15 minutes.
- Cook time: 30 minutes.

Ingredients

- 1/2 pound of ground beef.
- 1/2-pound ground beef heart.
- 1/2-pound ground beef liver.
- Three big eggs.
- 2 tablespoons beef tallow or butter.
- Salt to taste.

Instructions

- Preheat the oven to 350°F/175°C.
- In a skillet over medium heat, melt the beef tallow or butter. Combine the ground beef, beef heart, and beef liver. Cook for approximately 5-7 minutes, or until browned.
- In a mixing bowl, whisk the eggs with a pinch of salt.
- In a bowl, combine the cooked meat and eggs and mix thoroughly.
- Transfer the mixture to a lightly oiled 9-inch pie pan.
- Bake for 20-25 minutes, or until the eggs have set and the top is golden brown.
- Allow it cool for few minutes before slicing and serving.

Nutritional Information: Calories: 350; Protein: 30g; Fat: 25g; Carbohydrates: 1g.

Pork Belly and Egg Scramble

- Servings: Two.
- Prep time: 5 minutes.
- Cook time: 25 minutes.

Ingredients

- 1 pound (450 grams) pork belly, cut into 1/2-inch-thick slices
- Six big eggs.
- 2 tablespoons heavy cream.
- 2 tablespoons unsalted butter.
- Add salt and pepper to taste.

Instructions

- Cook in a large skillet over medium heat. Season the pork belly slices with salt and pepper.
- Cook the pork belly in the skillet for 5-7 minutes per side, until golden brown and crispy. Transfer to a platter and cover to stay heated.
- In a bowl, combine the eggs, heavy cream, salt, and pepper.
- In the same skillet, melt the butter over low heat. Pour in the egg mixture and simmer slowly, stirring regularly, until softly set.
- Serve the scrambled eggs with the crispy pork belly.

Nutritional Information: 500 calories, 30g of protein, 40g of fat, and 1g of carbohydrates.

Carnivore Breakfast Sandwich

- Servings: Two.
- Prep time: 10 minutes.
- Cooking Time: 10 minutes.

Ingredients

- Four sausage patties.
- Four big eggs.
- Two slices of cheese (optional).
- 2 tablespoons butter.

Instructions

- Cook in a skillet over medium heat. Cook the sausage patties until golden brown and thoroughly cooked, about 4-5 minutes per side. Remove and set aside.
- In the same skillet, melt the butter. Crack the eggs into the skillet and cook until desired doneness (sunny side up, over easy, etc.).
- To make the sandwich, place one sausage patty on a platter and top with an egg, a piece of cheese (if using), and another sausage patty.
- Repeat with the second sandwich. Serve hot.

Nutritional Information: Calories: 450; Protein: 30g; Fat: 35g; Carbohydrates: 1g.

Beef Liver Pâté with Carnivore Bread

- Serves: 4
- Prep time: 15 minutes.
- Cooking Time: 10 minutes.

Ingredients

- 1/2 pound of beef liver, trimmed and divided into little pieces
- 2.5 ounces unsalted butter.
- Salt to taste.
- Four slices of carnivore bread (made with ground beef, eggs, and cream cheese).

Instructions

- Melt the butter in a medium-sized pan over medium heat.
- Cook the beef liver chunks for 5-6 minutes, or until they are no longer pink.
- Place the cooked liver and melted butter in a food processor. Blend until smooth. Add salt to taste.
- Spread liver pâté on pieces of carnivorous bread.
- Serve immediately or chill until ready to use.

Nutritional Information: Calories: 300; Protein: 25g; Fat: 20g; Carbohydrates: 1g.

Bacon and Egg Cups

- Serving size: 6 cups
- Prep time: 10 minutes.
- Cook time: 20 minutes.

Ingredients

- Six pieces of bacon
- Six big eggs.
- Add salt and pepper to taste.

Instructions

• Preheat the oven to 375°F (190° C). Grease a muffin tray with a little butter or tallow.

• Line each muffin cup with a slice of bacon to create a cup shape.

• Crack one egg into each bacon-lined cup. Season with salt and pepper.

• Bake for 15-20 minutes, or until the eggs are cooked to your desired level.

• Allow to cool slightly before removing from the muffin tray. Serve warm.

Nutritional Information: Calories: 150; Protein: 12g; Fat: 11g; Carbohydrates: 1g.

CHAPTER 3: LUNCH.

Grilled Mediterranean Lamb Chops.

- Serves: 4
- Prep time: 10 minutes.
- Cooking Time: 10 minutes.

Ingredients

- Eight lamb chops.
- 2 tablespoons olive oil.
- 2 garlic cloves, minced
- One teaspoon of dried oregano.
- One teaspoon dried thyme.
- One teaspoon of salt.
- 1/2 teaspoon black pepper.
- Juice from 1 lemon

Instructions

- In a bowl, combine olive oil, garlic, oregano, thyme, salt, pepper, and lemon juice.
- Rub the mixture all over the lamb chops and let them marinate for at least 30 minutes.
- Preheat the grill to medium-high heat.
- Grill the lamb chops for 4-5 minutes per side, or until cooked to your liking.
- Allow the lamb chops to rest for a few minutes before serving.

Nutritional Information: Calories: 300; Protein: 25g; Fat: 22g; Carbohydrates: 1g.

Beef Heart Tacos

- Serves: 4
- Prep time: 15 minutes.
- Cooking Time: 10 minutes.

Ingredients

- 1 pound of beef heart, trimmed and diced
- 2 tablespoons beef tallow or lard.
- One teaspoon ground cumin
- One teaspoon of dried oregano.
- Add salt and pepper to taste.
- 8 large lettuce leaves (to wrap)

Instructions

- Melt the beef tallow or fat in a skillet over medium-high heat.
- Cook the diced beef heart for about 5-7 minutes, until browned and tender.
- Season with oregano, cumin, salt, and pepper.
- Serve the beef heart in large lettuce leaves as wraps.

Nutritional Information: Calories: 200; Protein: 30g; Fat: 10g; Carbohydrates: 1g.

Chicken Liver Pâté

- Servings: Six.
- Prep time: 10 minutes.
- Cook time: 20 minutes.

Ingredients

- 1 pound of trimmed chicken livers
- 1/2 cup of unsalted butter.
- 1 small onion, coarsely chopped
- 2 garlic cloves, minced
- One-quarter cup heavy cream
- Add salt and pepper to taste.

Instructions

- Melt 1/4 cup butter in a pan over medium heat.
- Cook the onion and garlic until softened, about 5 minutes.
- Cook the chicken livers until no longer pink in the center, about 10 minutes.
- Transfer the mixture to a food processor, then add the remaining butter and heavy cream. Blend until smooth.
- Add salt and pepper to taste.
- Place in a serving dish and chill until hard.

Nutritional Information: Calories: 250; Protein: 20g; Fat: 18g; Carbohydrates: 2g.

Pork Belly Salad

- Serves: 4
- Prep time: 15 minutes.
- Cook time: 20 minutes.

Ingredients

- Cut 1 pound pork belly into bite-sized pieces.
- 2 tablespoons olive oil.
- Add salt and pepper to taste.
- Four cups of mixed greens
- 1/4 cup crumbled blue cheese (optional).
- Two tablespoons of apple cider vinegar.

Instructions

- Preheat the oven to 400°F (200° C).
- Toss the pork belly pieces in olive oil, salt, and pepper.
- Place the pork belly on a baking sheet and roast for 20 minutes, until crispy.
- In a large mixing bowl, combine the greens, crumbled blue cheese (if using), and apple cider vinegar.
- Top with crispy pork belly chunks and serve immediately.

Nutritional Information: Calories: 350; Protein: 20g; Fat: 30g; Carbohydrates: 2g.

Carnivore Meatballs

- Serves: 4
- Prep time: 10 minutes.
- Cook time: 20 minutes.

Ingredients

- One pound of ground beef
- 1/2-pound ground pork.
- One big egg.
- 1/4 cup of grated Parmesan cheese (optional)
- One teaspoon of salt.
- 1/2 teaspoon black pepper.

Instructions

- Preheat the oven to 375°F (190° C).
- In a large mixing bowl, combine the ground beef, ground pork, egg, Parmesan cheese (if desired), salt, and pepper. Mix well.
- Shape the mixture into meatballs measuring about 1 inch in diameter.
- Place the meatballs on a baking sheet and bake for 20 minutes, or until thoroughly cooked.
- Serve hot.

Nutritional Information: Calories: 300; Protein: 25g; Fat: 22g; Carbohydrates: 1g.

Beef Tongue Tacos

- Serves: 4
- Prep time: 15 minutes.
- Cook time: three hours.

Ingredients

- 1 beef tongue (about 2-3 pounds)
- One large, quartered onion
- 4 garlic cloves, peeled
- Two bay leaves.
- Salt to taste.
- Large lettuce leaves (to wrap)

Instructions

- Put the beef tongue in a big pot and cover it with water. Add the onion, garlic, bay leaves, and plenty of salt.
- Bring to a boil, then decrease heat and simmer for approximately 3 hours, or until the tongue is soft.
- Remove the tongue from the pot and allow to cool somewhat. Peel off and discard the outer layer.
- Cut the tongue into tiny strips.
- Serve the sliced tongue in large lettuce leaves as wraps.

Nutritional Information: Calories: 250; Protein: 30g; Fat: 15g; Carbohydrates: 1g.

Lamb and Eggplant Skewers

- Serves: 4
- Prep time: 15 minutes.
- Cook time: 15 minutes.

Ingredients

- Cut 1 lb. lamb into 1-inch cubes.
- 1 large eggplant, cut into 1-inch cubes.
- 2 tablespoons olive oil.
- One teaspoon of dried oregano.
- One teaspoon dried thyme.
- Add salt and pepper to taste.
- Soak wooden skewers in water for 30 minutes

Instructions

- In a bowl, mix together the olive oil, oregano, thyme, salt, and pepper. Add the lamb and eggplant cubes and stir to combine.
- Thread the lamb and eggplant onto the skewers, rotating between them.
- Preheat the grill to medium-high heat.
- Grill the skewers for 10-15 minutes, rotating regularly, until the lamb is cooked to your liking and the eggplant is soft.
- Serve hot.

Nutritional Information: Calories: 300; Protein: 25g; Fat: 20g; Carbohydrates: 5g.

Carnivore's Chicken Salad

- Serves: 4
- Prep time: 10 minutes.

Ingredients

- 2 cups of cooked chicken, shredded
- 1/2 cup mayonnaise (ideally homemade and carnivore-friendly)
- Two hardboiled eggs, chopped
- Add salt and pepper to taste.

Instructions

- In a large mixing bowl, combine the shredded chicken, mayonnaise, and chopped hard-boiled eggs.
- Add salt and pepper to taste.
- Mix thoroughly until all components are equally covered.
- Serve immediately, or chill until ready to eat.

Nutritional Information: Calories: 350; Protein: 30g; Fat: 25g; Carbohydrates: 1g.

Beef & Bone Marrow Soup

- Serves: 4
- Prep time: 15 minutes.
- Cooking Time: 4 hours.

Ingredients

- 2-pound beef shank with bone marrow
- One large, quartered onion
- 4 garlic cloves, peeled
- Two bay leaves.
- Add salt and pepper to taste.
- Water to cover.

Instructions

- Put the beef shank in a big pot and cover it with water. Combine the onion, garlic, bay leaves, salt, and pepper.
- Bring to a boil, then reduce to a simmer for approximately 4 hours, or until the meat is cooked and the marrow is soft.
- Remove the beef shank from the pot. Scoop the marrow out of the bones and return it to the saucepan.
- Shred the meat and add it to the pot as well.
- Adjust seasoning with salt and pepper as needed.
- Serve hot.

Nutritional Information: Calories: 400; Protein: 30g; Fat: 30g; Carbohydrates: 2g.

Pork Rind Nachos

- Serves: 4
- Prep time: 10 minutes.
- Cooking Time: 10 minutes.

Ingredients

- Four cups of plain pork rinds
- One cup shredded cheddar cheese.
- 1/2 cup of cooked ground beef.
- 1/4 cup sour cream.
- 1/4 cup sliced jalapeños (optional).

Instructions

- Preheat the oven to 375°F (190° C).
- Spread the pork rinds onto a baking sheet.
- Distribute the shredded cheddar cheese and cooked ground beef evenly over the pork rinds.
- Bake for 5-10 minutes, or until the cheese melts and bubbles.
- Serve with sour cream and optional sliced jalapeños after baking.
- Serve immediately.

Nutritional Information: Calories: 350; Protein: 25g; Fat: 25g; Carbohydrates: 2g.

CHAPTER 4: DINNER

One-Pan Honey-Glazed Brisket

- Servings: Six.
- Prep time: 15 minutes.
- Cooking Time: 4-5 hours.

Ingredients

- One whole beef brisket (5-6 pounds)
- One cup honey.
- 1/2 cup soy sauce (or coconut aminos for a soy-free alternative)
- One-quarter cup olive oil
- 4 garlic cloves, minced
- One teaspoon of ground ginger
- One teaspoon of paprika
- Add salt and black pepper to taste.

Instructions

- Preheat the oven to 300°F (150° C).
- In a bowl, combine the honey, soy sauce, olive oil, minced garlic, ground ginger, and paprika.
- Season the brisket well with salt and black pepper, then transfer it to a large roasting pan.
- Pour the honey glaze over the brisket, making sure it's uniformly coated on both sides.

- Wrap the roasting pan snugly in aluminum foil and place it in the preheated oven.
- Cook the brisket for 4-5 hours, basting regularly with pan juices.
- After the initial cooking time, remove the foil and raise the oven temperature to 400°F (200°C).
- Roast the brisket uncovered for another 30-40 minutes, or until the glaze caramelizes and the meat is tender and moist.
- After cooking, take the brisket from the oven and let it rest for 10-15 minutes before slicing. Serve hot.

Nutritional Information: Calories: 450, Protein: 35g, Fat: 25g, Carbs: 20g.

White Sauce Zucchini Lasagna

- Servings: Six.
- Prep time: 20 minutes.
- Cook time: 40 minutes.

Ingredients

- 4 medium zucchinis, cut lengthwise into thin strips.
- One pound of ground beef
- One cup of ricotta cheese
- One cup shredded mozzarella cheese.
- 1/2 cup of grated Parmesan cheese.
- One cup heavy cream.
- 2 garlic cloves, minced
- Add salt and pepper to taste.

Instructions

- Preheat the oven to 375°F (190° C).
- Cook the ground beef in a pan over medium heat until browned. Drain any extra fat.
- In a bowl, combine the ricotta, half of the mozzarella, half of the Parmesan, heavy cream, minced garlic, salt, and pepper.
- In a baking dish, layer the zucchini pieces, ground beef, and cheese mixture, repeating until all ingredients are used, then finish with a layer of cheese.
- Add the remaining mozzarella and Parmesan cheese over top.
- Bake for 30-40 minutes, or until the cheese is melted and golden brown.
- Cool for a few minutes before serving.

Nutritional Information: Calories: 400; Protein: 30g; Fat: 30g; Carbohydrates: 5g.

Roasted Duck with Orange Glaze

- Serves: 4
- Prep time: 15 minutes.
- Cook Time: 2.5 hours.

Ingredients

- One whole duck (5-6 pounds).
- 1/2 cup of orange juice.
- One-quarter cup honey
- 2 tablespoons soy sauce (or coconut aminos for a soy-free alternative)
- One tablespoon olive oil.
- 2 garlic cloves, minced

- Add salt and pepper to taste.

Instructions

- Preheat the oven to 350°F/175°C.
- Rinse the duck inside and out, then wipe dry with paper towels. Season the duck well with salt and pepper.
- In a mixing bowl, combine orange juice, honey, soy sauce, olive oil, and minced garlic.
- Put the duck on a rack in a roasting pan. Brush the duck with the orange glaze.
- Roast the duck in a preheated oven for approximately 2.5 hours, basting every 30 minutes with the leftover glaze.
- Raise the oven temperature to 400°F (200°C) for the final 30 minutes to crisp the skin.
- Allow the duck to rest for 10 to 15 minutes before carving. Serve hot.

Nutritional Information: Calories: 500; Protein: 35g; Fat: 35g; Carbohydrates: 10g.

Braised Short Ribs.

- Serves: 4
- Prep time: 15 minutes.
- Cook time: three hours.

Ingredients

- 4 pounds of beef short ribs.
- Two cups of beef broth.
- One cup of red wine (optional).
- One large onion, chopped
- 4 garlic cloves, minced
- Add salt and pepper to taste.
- 2 tablespoons olive oil.

Instructions

- Preheat the oven to 325°F (165° C).
- Season the short ribs with a sufficient amount of salt and pepper.
- In a large Dutch oven, heat the olive oil on medium-high heat. Sear the short ribs on all sides until browned, about 2-3 minutes per side. Remove and set aside.
- In the same pot, combine the chopped onion and garlic. Cook for approximately 5 minutes, or until softened.
- Stir in the beef broth and red wine (if using), scraping up any browned pieces from the bottom of the pot.
- Return the short ribs to the saucepan, cover, and put into the preheated oven.
- Braise for approximately 3 hours, or until the meat is tender and falling off the bone.

- Remove the short ribs from the pot and allow them rest for a few minutes before serving. Serve hot.

Nutritional information: calories: 600, protein: 45g, fat: 45g, carbs: 5g

Carnivore Meatloaf

- Servings: Six.
- Prep time: 10 minutes.
- Cook time: one hour.

Ingredients

- 1.5 pounds of ground beef.
- One cup crushed pork rinds.
- One big egg.
- 1/2 cup of grated Parmesan cheese.
- One teaspoon of salt.
- 1/2 teaspoon black pepper.

Instructions

- Preheat the oven to 350°F/175°C.
- In a large mixing bowl, combine ground beef, crushed pork rinds, egg, Parmesan cheese, salt, and pepper. Mix well.
- Form the mixture into a loaf and place in a loaf pan or on a baking sheet.
- Bake for 1 hour, or until the meatloaf is thoroughly cooked and a meat thermometer reads 160°F (70°C).
- Allow the meatloaf to rest for ten minutes before slicing. Serve hot.

Nutritional Information: Calories: 400; Protein: 30g; Fat: 30g; Carbohydrates: 1g.

Beef Wellington

- Servings: Six.
- Prep time: 30 minutes.
- Cook time: one hour.

Ingredients

- 2-pound beef tenderloin
- 1/2-pound prosciutto
- 1/2-pound mushrooms, finely chopped
- 2 tablespoons butter.
- 2 tablespoons Dijon mustard.
- One egg, beaten
- Add salt and pepper to taste.

Instructions

- Preheat the oven to 400°F (200° C).
- Season the beef tenderloin with salt and pepper. Sear it in a hot pan with butter until golden on all sides. Let it cool before brushing with Dijon mustard.
- Cook the mushrooms in the same pan until they lose moisture and become dry. Let it cool.
- Arrange the prosciutto slices on a sheet of plastic wrap, overlapping slightly. Spread the mushroom mixture on the prosciutto.
- Place the beef tenderloin on top and roll it securely with the plastic wrap. Chill in the fridge for 15 minutes.

- Roll the puff pastry out on a floured surface. Remove the plastic wrap from the steak and arrange it in the middle of the pastry. Wrap the pastry around the steak and secure the edges.
- Brush the pastry with beaten egg, then arrange the wrapped meat on a baking sheet.
- Bake for 25-30 minutes, until the pastry is golden brown and the beef is cooked to your liking.
- Rest for 10 minutes before slicing and serving.

Nutritional Information: Calories: 600; Protein: 40g; Fat: 45g; Carbohydrates: 10g.

Grilled Rib Eye Steak

- Servings: Two.
- Prep time: 10 minutes.
- Cooking Time: 10 minutes.

Ingredients

- Two ribeye steaks (about 1 inch thick)
- 2 tablespoons olive oil.
- Add salt and pepper to taste.
- 2 tablespoons butter.

Instructions

- Preheat the grill to high heat.
- Coat the steaks with olive oil and season generously with salt and pepper.
- Place the steaks on the grill and cook for 4-5 minutes per side for medium-rare, or until done to your liking.
- Remove the steaks from the grill and allow them to rest for 5 minutes.
- Before serving, top each steak with a pat of butter.

Nutritional Information: Calories: 700; Protein: 50g; Fat: 55g; Carbohydrates: 0g.

Carnivore Pizza

- Serves: 4
- Prep time: 15 minutes.
- Cook time: 20 minutes.

Ingredients

- One pound of ground chicken.
- 1 egg
- 1/2 cup of grated Parmesan cheese.
- One cup shredded mozzarella cheese.
- 1/2 cup cooked bacon, crumbled
- Salt to taste.

Instructions

- Preheat the oven to 400°F (200° C).
- In a mixing bowl, combine the ground chicken, egg, and Parmesan cheese thoroughly.
- Form a pizza crust by spreading the ingredients onto a baking sheet coated with parchment.
- Bake for 15 minutes, or until the crust is firm and lightly brown.
- Remove from the oven and sprinkle with shredded mozzarella and crumbled bacon.
- Return to the oven and bake for 5 more minutes, or until the cheese is melted and bubbling.
- Cool slightly before slicing and serving.

Nutritional Information: Calories: 400; Protein: 35g; Fat: 25g; Carbohydrates: 1g.

Stuffed Pork Tenderloin

- Serves: 4
- Prep time: 20 minutes.
- Cook time: 40 minutes.

Ingredients

- 1 pork tenderloin (about 1.5 pounds)
- 1/2 cup cooked bacon, crumbled
- 1/2 cup shredded mozzarella cheese.
- 2 tablespoons butter.
- Add salt and pepper to taste.

Instructions

- Preheat the oven to 375°F (190° C).
- Butterfly the pork tenderloin by slicing it lengthwise, taking care not to go all the way through. Open it like a book.
- Season the insides with salt and pepper. Spread the crumbled bacon and shredded mozzarella cheese equally across the surface.
- Roll up the tenderloin and fasten with kitchen twine.
- In a skillet, melt the butter over medium-high heat. Sear the tenderloin on all sides until golden.
- Place the tenderloin on a baking dish and cook for 25-30 minutes, or until the internal temperature reaches 145°F (63°C).
- Rest for 10 minutes before slicing and serving.

Nutritional Information: Calories: 350; Protein: 40g; Fat: 20g; Carbohydrates: 1g.

Lamb Shank Stew

- Serves: 4
- Prep time: 15 minutes.
- Cook time: three hours.

Ingredients

- Four lamb shanks.
- Two cups of bone broth.
- Two tablespoons tallow or butter
- Add salt and pepper to taste.

Instructions

- Preheat the oven to 325°F (165° C).
- Season the lamb shanks with salt and pepper.
- In a large Dutch oven, melt the tallow or butter over medium-high heat. Sear the lamb shanks on all sides until brown.
- Place the bone broth in the pot and heat to a boil.
- Cover the pot and place it in the preheated oven.
- Braise for approximately 3 hours, or until the lamb shanks are tender and falling off the bone.
- Serve hot.

Nutritional Information: Calories: 500; Protein: 40g; Fat: 35g; Carbohydrates: 1g.

CHAPTER 5: SNACKS.

Bone Marrow Butter

- Serves: 4
- Prep time: 10 minutes.
- Cook time: 20 minutes.

Ingredients

- Four marrow bones.
- 1/2 cup unsalted butter, softened
- Salt to taste.

Instructions

- Preheat the oven to 450°F (230°C).
- Place the marrow bones on a baking sheet and roast for 15-20 minutes, until tender and slightly puffed.
- Scoop the marrow off the bones and place it in a basin. Allow it to cool somewhat.
- Place the softened butter and a pinch of salt in the bowl. Mix until thoroughly blended and smooth.
- Place the bone marrow butter in a shallow dish and chill until solid.
- Spread on carnivorous bread or use as a topping for steaks.

Nutritional Information: Calories: 200; Protein: 2g; Fat: 22g; Carbohydrates: 0g.

Pork Rinds

- Serves: 4
- Prep time: 10 minutes.
- Cook time: 20 minutes.

Ingredients

- One pound of pork skin.
- Salt to taste.

Instructions

- Preheat the oven to 400°F (200° C).
- Chop the pig skin into small pieces.
- Arrange the pig skin pieces on a baking sheet in a single layer.
- Bake for 15-20 minutes, or until the pig rinds get crispy and golden brown.
- Remove from the oven and season with salt to taste.
- Let cool before serving.

Nutritional Information: Calories: 150; Protein: 10g; Fat: 12g; Carbohydrates: 0g.

Beef Jerky

- Servings: Six.
- Prep time: 15 minutes.
- Cooking Time: 4 hours.

Ingredients

- 2 pounds flank steak, thinly sliced
- One tablespoon of salt.
- One teaspoon of black pepper.
- One teaspoon garlic powder.

Instructions

- Preheat the oven to 175°F (80° C).
- In a bowl, add the salt, black pepper, and garlic powder.
- Toss the cut meat in the spice mixture until thoroughly coated.
- Place the beef slices on a baking sheet in a single layer.
- Bake for about 4 hours, or until the beef is dry and chewy.
- Allow to cool before storing in an airtight container.

Nutritional Information: Calories: 200; Protein: 30g; Fat: 8g; Carbohydrates: 0g.

Cheese Stuffed Meatballs

- Serves: 4
- Prep time: 15 minutes.
- Cook time: 20 minutes.

Ingredients

- One pound of ground beef
- 1/2 cup shredded mozzarella cheese.
- One big egg.
- 1/4 cup grated parmesan cheese.
- Add salt and pepper to taste.

Instructions

- Preheat the oven to 375°F (190° C).
- In a bowl, mix together the ground beef, egg, Parmesan cheese, salt, and pepper. Mix well.
- Shape the mixture into small meatballs of about 1 inch in diameter.
- Place a little quantity of shredded mozzarella cheese in the center of each meatball and seal the meat around it.
- Place the meatballs on a baking sheet and bake for 20 minutes, or until thoroughly cooked.
- Serve hot.

Nutritional Information: Calories: 300; Protein: 25g; Fat: 20g; Carbohydrates: 1g.

Carnivore Chips

- Serves: 4
- Prep time: 10 minutes.
- Cook time: one hour.

Ingredients

- 1 pound beef, thinly sliced
- 1/2 teaspoon salt.
- 1/2 teaspoon black pepper.

Instructions

- Preheat the air fryer to 200°F (95°C).
- Season the thinly sliced meat with salt and black pepper.
- Place the beef slices in a single layer in the air fryer basket.
- Air fried for approximately 55 minutes, or until the beef is crispy.
- Let cool before serving.

Nutritional Information: Calories: 150, Protein: 25g, Fat: 5g, Carbs: 0g.

Bacon- Wrapped Dates

- Serves: 4
- Prep time: 10 minutes.
- Cook time: 20 minutes.

Ingredients

- 12 big Medjool dates, pitted
- Twelve pieces of bacon.

Instructions

- Preheat the oven to 400°F (200° C).
- Wrap each pitted date with a slice of bacon and secure with a toothpick.
- Arrange the bacon-wrapped dates on a baking sheet coated with parchment paper.
- Bake the bacon for 15-20 minutes, or until crispy.
- Allow to cool somewhat before serving.

Nutritional Information: Calories: 150, Protein: 5g, Fat: 10g, Carbs: 10g.

Carnivore Bars

- Servings: eight bars.
- Prep time: 10 minutes.
- Cooking Time: 4 hours.

Ingredients

- One pound of ground beef
- 1/2 cup of beef tallow.
- Salt to taste.

Instructions

- Preheat the oven to 200°F (95° C).
- Cook the ground beef in a pan over medium heat until thoroughly done. Drain any extra fat.
- Place the cooked ground beef on a baking sheet in a thin layer.
- Dehydrate in the oven for 3-4 hours, or until the meat is dry and crispy.
- Melt the beef tallow in a saucepan over low heat.
- Combine the desiccated beef, melted tallow, and salt.
- Place the mixture in a baking dish and chill until hard.
- Cut into bars and keep in the fridge.

Nutritional Information: Calories: 250; Protein: 20g; Fat: 20g; Carbohydrates: 0g.

Chicken Skin Cracklings

- Serves: 4
- Prep time: 10 minutes.
- Cook time: 40 minutes.

Ingredients

- One pound of chicken skin.
- Salt to taste.

Instructions

- Preheat the oven to 400°F (200° C).
- Place the chicken skin flat on a baking sheet lined with parchment paper.
- Season with salt.
- Bake for 30-40 minutes, or until the skin turns crispy and golden brown.
- Let cool before serving.

Nutritional Information: Calories: 150; Protein: 10g; Fat: 12g; Carbohydrates: 0g.

Carnivore Deviled Eggs

- Servings: Six.
- Prep time: 10 minutes.
- Cook time: 15 minutes.

Ingredients

- Six big eggs.
- 1/4 cup mayonnaise (ideally homemade or carnivore-friendly)
- Two pieces of cooked and crumbled bacon
- Salt to taste.

Instructions

- Pour the eggs into a pot and cover with water. Bring to a boil over medium high heat.
- Once boiling, remove from the heat and cover. Let it sit for 11 minutes.
- Drain the hot water and rinse the eggs under cold running water. Peel the eggs.
- Cut the eggs in half lengthwise, then remove the yolks.
- In a bowl, combine the yolks, mayonnaise, and salt and mash until smooth.
- Pour or pour the yolk mixture back into the egg whites.
- Garnish with crumbled bacon and serve.

Nutritional Information: Calories: 100; Protein: 6g; Fat: 8g; Carbohydrates: 1g.

Beef Fat Bombs

- Servings: eight.
- Prep time: 10 minutes.

Ingredients

- 1 cup beef tallow, melted
- 1/2 cup of beef protein powder.
- Salt to taste.

Instructions

- In a bowl, combine the melted beef tallow, beef protein powder, and salt until well blended.
- Transfer the mixture to silicone molds or a baking dish.
- Chill until hard, about 1-2 hours.
- Remove the fat bombs from their molds or, if using a baking dish, cut them into squares.
- Keep in the fridge until ready to eat.

Nutritional Information: Calories: 250; Protein: 10g; Fat: 22g; Carbohydrates: 0g.

CHAPTER 6: DESSERTS

Yogurt Cheesecake with Blueberry and Lemon Compote

- Servings: eight.
- Prep time: 20 minutes.
- Cook time is 1 hour (plus chilling time).

Ingredients

For cheesecake:

- Two cups of full-fat Greek yogurt
- 2 cups softened cream cheese.
- Three big eggs.
- One-half cup honey
- 1 teaspoon of vanilla extract.

For the blueberry-lemon compote:

- One cup blueberry.
- One-quarter cup water
- One tablespoon of lemon juice.
- 1 tablespoon honey.

Instructions

- Preheat oven: Set the oven to 325°F (160°C). Grease a 9-inch springform pan.

- Make the Cheesecake Mixture: In a large bowl, mix the cream cheese until smooth. Mix in the Greek yogurt, honey, and vanilla essence until thoroughly blended. Add the eggs one at a time, beating thoroughly after each addition.
- Bake Cheesecake: Transfer the mixture to the prepared pan. Bake for 50 to 60 minutes, or until the middle is set. Allow it cool until room temperature, then refrigerate for at least 4 hours or overnight.
- Make the compote: In a small saucepan, combine the blueberries, water, lemon juice, and honey. Cook for about 10 minutes on medium heat, or until the blueberries burst and the mixture thickens. Let it cool.
- To serve, top the chilled cheesecake with the blueberry-lemon compote.

Nutritional Information: Calories: 300. Protein: 10g, fat: 20g, carbohydrates: 20g.

Honey-Glazed Bacon

- Serves: 4
- Prep time: 5 minutes.
- Cook time: 20 minutes.

Ingredients

- Twelve pieces of bacon.
- One-quarter cup honey
- 1/2 teaspoon of black pepper (optional)

Instructions

- Preheat Oven: Set your oven to 375°F (190°C). Line a baking sheet with parchment paper.
- Prepare Bacon: Place the bacon slices on a baking sheet. Brush honey over each slice and, if desired, sprinkle with black pepper.
- Bake: Cook for 15-20 minutes, or until the bacon is crispy and caramelized.
- Cool: Allow the bacon to cool on a wire rack before serving.

Nutritional Information: Calories: 200. Protein: 10g, fat: 15g, carbohydrates: 10g.

Creamy Egg Custard

- Serves: 4
- Prep time: 10 minutes.
- Cook time: 40 minutes.

Ingredients

- Six big eggs.
- 1 1/2 cup heavy cream.
- 1 teaspoon of vanilla extract.
- 1/4 cup of honey (optional)
- A pinch of salt.

Instructions

- Preheat oven: Set your oven to 350°F (175°C).
- Make the Custard Mixture: In a bowl, mix together the eggs, heavy cream, vanilla extract, honey (if using), and salt until thoroughly incorporated.

- Bake Custard: Transfer the mixture to ramekins. Place the ramekins in a baking dish and fill with hot water to about halfway up the sides.
- Bake for 35-40 minutes, or until the custard is firm but somewhat jiggly in the center.
- Cool: Remove the ramekins from the water bath and allow to cool. Refrigerate for a minimum of 2 hours before serving.

Nutritional Information: 250 calories, 6g protein, 22g fat, and 10g carbohydrates.

Carnivore Ice Cream.

- Serves: 4
- Prep time: 10 minutes.
- Cooking Time: 10 minutes (plus freezing time).

Ingredients

- Three large egg yolks.
- 1-1/2 cups heavy whipping cream
- 1 teaspoon of vanilla extract.
- Two tablespoons honey (optional)

Instructions

- Prepare the mixture by heating the heavy whipping cream in a saucepan over medium heat until it begins to simmer. In a separate dish, whisk together the egg yolks until creamy.
- Combine: Gradually add the hot cream into the egg yolks while whisking constantly to prevent curdling. Return the mixture to the saucepan and

simmer on low heat, stirring frequently, until thick enough to coat the back of a spoon.

- Add Flavor: Remove from the heat and mix in the vanilla essence and honey (if using).
- Freeze: Put the mixture in a jar and freeze for at least 4 hours, stirring every 30 minutes to keep ice crystals from forming.
- Scoop and serve once completely frozen.

Nutritional Information: Calories: 350; protein: 5g; fat: 35g; carbohydrates: 10g.

Beef Tallow Brownies

- Servings: eight.
- Prep time: 15 minutes.
- Cook time: 25 minutes.

Ingredients

- 1/2 cup beef tallow, melted
- Three big eggs.
- 1/2 cup of cocoa powder.
- One-half cup honey
- 1 teaspoon of vanilla extract.
- A pinch of salt.

Instructions

- Preheat oven: Set your oven to 350°F (175°C). Grease an 8-by-8-inch baking pan.
- Make the batter: In a mixing bowl, combine the melted beef tallow, eggs, cocoa powder, honey, vanilla extract, and salt. Whisk until smooth.
- Bake: Transfer the batter to the prepared pan and distribute evenly.
- Bake for 20 to 25 minutes, or until a toothpick inserted in the center comes out clean.
- Cool: Allow the brownies to cool in their pan before cutting into squares and serving.

Nutritional Information: 250 calories, 5g protein, 20g fat, and 15g carbohydrates.

Carnivore Chocolate Mousse

- Serves: 4
- Prep time: 10 minutes.

Ingredients

- 1 cup of heavy cream, cool
- 1/2 cup unsweetened cocoa powder.
- 1/4 cup of honey (optional)
- 1/2 teaspoon vanilla extract.
- A pinch of salt.

Instructions

- In a large basin, whisk the heavy cream until firm peaks form.
- In a separate mixing bowl, combine the cocoa powder, honey (if using), vanilla essence, and salt.
- Gently whisk the chocolate mixture into the whipped cream until well mixed.
- Transfer the mousse to serving glasses or bowls.
- Chill for at least two hours before serving.

Nutritional Information: Calories: 250, protein: 3g, fat: 22g, carbohydrates: 15g.

Bacon Fat Shortbread Cookies.

- Serving size: 12 cookies.
- Prep time: 15 minutes.
- Cook time: 20 minutes.

Ingredients

- One cup of almond flour.
- 1/4 cup melted bacon grease.
- 1/4 cup softened butter.
- 1/4 cup of honey (optional)
- 1/2 teaspoon vanilla extract.
- A pinch of salt.

Instructions

- Preheat the oven to 350°F/175°C. Line a baking sheet with parchment paper.
- In a mixing bowl, combine the almond flour, bacon grease, butter, honey (if using), vanilla essence, and salt until the dough forms.
- Form the dough into tiny balls and place on the prepared baking sheet. Flatten each ball slightly with your palm or a fork.
- Bake for 15-20 minutes, or until the sides turn golden brown.
- Cool the cookies on the baking sheet before transferring them to a wire rack.

Nutritional Information: 150 calories, 3g protein, 14g fat, and 5g carbohydrates.

Carnivore Panna Cotta

- Serves: 4
- Prep time: 10 minutes.

Ingredients

- Two cups of heavy cream.
- One tablespoon gelatin
- One-quarter cup water
- 1 teaspoon of vanilla extract.
- Two tablespoons honey (optional)

Instructions

- In a small bowl, sprinkle the gelatin over the water and set aside for 5 minutes to bloom.
- In a saucepan, heat the heavy cream over medium heat until it starts to simmer. Don't boil.

- Remove from the heat and mix in the bloomed gelatin until completely dissolved.
- Combine the vanilla extract and honey (if using) and blend thoroughly.
- Transfer the mixture to ramekins or serving glasses.
- Chill for at least four hours, or until set.
- Serve cold.

Nutritional Information: Calories: 300, protein: 5g, fat: 28g, carbohydrates: 10g.

Pork Rind Cinnamon Rolls

- Servings: Six.
- Prep time: 20 minutes.
- Cook time: 25 minutes.

Ingredients

- Two cups crushed pork rinds.
- One-half cup almond flour
- 1/4 cup melted butter.
- Two big eggs.
- 1/4 cup of honey (optional)
- One teaspoon of cinnamon.
- 1/2 teaspoon baking powder.

Instructions

- Preheat the oven to 350°F/175°C. Grease a baking dish.
- In a mixing bowl, combine the crushed pork rinds, almond flour, melted butter, eggs, honey (if using), cinnamon, and baking powder until the dough forms.
- On a piece of parchment paper, roll the dough into a rectangular shape.
- Add extra melted butter and cinnamon to the dough.
- Roll the dough into a log and cut it into 1-inch slices.
- Transfer the pieces to the prepared baking tray.
- Bake for 20–25 minutes, or until golden brown.
- Allow to cool somewhat before serving.

Nutritional Information: Calories: 200. Protein: 10g, fat: 15g, carbohydrates: 5g.

Carnivore Lemon Bars

- Servings: eight.
- Prep time: 15 minutes.
- Cook time: 25 minutes.

Ingredients

For the crust:

- One cup of almond flour.
- 1/4 cup melted butter.
- One tablespoon honey (optional)

For filling:

- Four big eggs.
- 1/2 cup of lemon juice.
- 1/4 cup of honey (optional)
- One-quarter cup heavy cream

Instructions

- Preheat the oven to 350°F/175°C. Line an 8-by-8-inch baking dish with parchment paper.
- Make the Crust: In a bowl, combine the almond flour, melted butter, and honey (if using) until well blended. Press the mixture into the bottom of the prepared baking dish.
- Bake for ten minutes, or until the crust is lightly brown. Remove from the oven and allow it cool slightly.
- Make the Filling: In a mixing bowl, whisk together the eggs, lemon juice, honey (if using), and heavy cream until smooth.
- Spread the filling over the prebaked crust.
- Bake for 15-20 minutes, until the filling has set.
- Allow to cool completely before cutting into bars and serving.

Nutritional Information: 250 calories, 6g protein, 20g fat, and 10g carbohydrates.

CHAPTER 7: BONUS SECTIONS.

7-Day Meal Plan

Day 1

- Breakfast: Carnivore Waffles.
- Lunch: Grilled Mediterranean lamb chops
- Dinner: One-Pan Honey-Glazed Brisket.
- Snack: Bone Marrow Butter.

Day 2

- Breakfast: Liver and Bacon Omelets
- Lunch - Beef Heart Tacos
- Dinner: White Sauce Zucchini Lasagna
- Snack: pork rinds.

Day 3

- Breakfast: Sausage and egg muffins.
- Lunch: Chicken liver pate.
- Dinner: Roasted duck with orange glaze.
- Snack: beef jerky.

Day 4

- Beef and Egg Breakfast Bowl
- Lunch - Pork Belly Salad
- Dinner: braised short ribs.
- Snack: Cheese-stuffed meatballs.

Day 5

- Breakfast: Creamy Shrimp with Eggs
- Lunch: Carnivore Meatballs.
- Dinner: Carnivore Meatloaf
- Snack: Carnivore chips.

Day 6

- Breakfast - Organ Meat Pie
- Lunch - Beef Tongue Tacos
- Dinner: Beef Wellington.
- Snack: Bacon Wrapped Dates

Day 7

- Breakfast: Pork belly and egg scramble.
- Lunch: lamb and eggplant skewers.
- Dinner: grilled ribeye steak.
- Snack: Carnivore bars.

CONCLUSION

Thank you for accompanying me on this culinary adventure into the realm of animal-based eating. I hope this cookbook has given you tasty meals, useful ideas, and motivation to adopt a diet that appreciates the richness and diversity of animal-based nutrition. From hearty breakfasts to filling dinners, savory snacks to decadent desserts, each meal is designed to fuel your body while also pleasing your taste buds.

As you continue to discover and enjoy these recipes, I invite you to experiment, adapt, and personalize them. The pleasure of cooking lies in its limitless potential, and I hope this cookbook serves as a springboard for your culinary imagination.

Your comment is really valuable to me. If you have enjoyed and found this cookbook useful, I would appreciate it if you could give a favorable review. Your honest input not only helps me improve future editions, but it also helps other readers learn about the benefits of an animal-based diet.

Thank you for your support, and happy cooking!

Made in the USA
Monee, IL
31 December 2024

75729497R00039